A Muse In Tunes

A Creative's Journal To Satisfaction

Created By: Budd Hansen

VEHICLEDIGEST PUBLISHING, LLC | PORTLAND, OREGON, USA

WWW.BUDDHANSEN.COM
WWW.VEHICLEDIGEST.NET

A MUSE IN TUNES

A CREATIVE'S JOURNAL TO SATISFACTION

PAPER BACK ISBN: 978-1-7332172-4-8
PAPER BACK ASIN: 173321724X

HARD COVER ISBN: 978-1-7332172-3-1
HARD COVER ASIN: 1733217231

COVER DESIGN BY: BUDD 'TK' HANSEN
EDITED BY: BUDD 'TK' HANSEN

WRITEME@BUDDHANSEN.COM

AN INTRODUCTION TO A CREATIVE WRITER'S MUSE

MUSIC: AN ABSTRACT CONNECTION BETWEEN THE 'SPACES' WE HUMANS MOVE INTO WHEN SOUND COMES ON—IS DRIVEN BY EMOTION THAT BRINGS US CLOSER TOGETHER AS IT PLAYS OUT CERTAIN FREQUENCIES. IN RETURN, WE FUNCTION OUT OF LOVE AMONGST PEOPLE WE COULD CARE LESS FOR ONCE THE MUSIC IS OFF. ALTHOUGH THERE IS AN AFTERSHOCK, THIS ILLUSTRATES A VEHICLE OF LOVE AND ARGUABLY THE KEY TO BRINGING THE HUMAN RACE TOGETHER AS ONE. BUT IT'S NOT ENOUGH BECAUSE WE FORGET AND MOVE ON. I WROTE 'BUDD'S SOUNDTRACK' IN ONE NIGHT AND EDITED IT OVER A WEEKEND AFTER LISTENING TO **HIPPO CAMPUS**' *NEW* ALBUM, 'BAMBI.'

Budd's Soundtrack: Volume I

October 2, 2018

Blinded by music as it takes us into our next journey of life, through a sequence of emotional episodes, we manifest memories of moments with family, time at work, and fun stuff. As a song takes you into retrograde, the recollection of thoughts allows you to appreciate that even in the worst of times, you've had time to think things over.

Time to think over decisions you made that were derived from emotions. But do most of us think in the NOW? Meaning, disregarding our emotional data, music may be a distraction. Ironically, lyrics have fuelled everything you'll read from here on.

Like a *passenger* in this world, riding on the roller-coasters of courage and DOPAMINE, music takes me there as well...

To where?

To places I wanna' make rash decisions.

Feeling music for the first time at an early age, I'm old enough to recall how Warren G. and Bone Thugs put me in their shoes. I didn't want to be them; maybe in the context of their music, I did, but like the rock music I listen to today, it triggers a compartment I have embedded deep within. It led me to configure where my emotions come from, why music emerges from irrational desires, and why I listen to everything…EVERYTHING. Luckily, no rash decisions were ever made listening to music—just my *body of a dancing eye*.

What's actually made is an emotional oath or feeling from the music influencing thoughts, painted pictures, and judgments of how I see the world through sound. Anything can sound so beautiful from what's derived from our thoughts, influenced by emotions, and carried out by the environment.

…but you must agree, okay?

Periodically, I go retrograde, ignoring the guilt because of my father's (mis) judgment of my music preference. But that's neither here nor there. Where is it exactly? It's where I turn the music down in my car so the elderly drivers pulling up next to me see me as one of the good ones.

Then I turn that shit back up because I'm usually giggin'…

Listening to the music my father grew up on and what empowered his lifestyle, I thought that for one genre of music to be assumed respected above the other, it doesn't mean it's better. As a preacher's son, I grew conflicted with this.

A genre, at best, portrays the diverse lifestyles of people who care to connect with it. Without categorizing those who listen, it's also the *people* who create the art, pictures, and noise, who are experiencing such illustrated emotions. The artists create what's appealing to the people, from what they envision, and more importantly, their unique abstract feelings to transpire into finite creations. If the art is inconsistent with the people over time, it likely dies within the community and becomes history.

With the appropriate influencers, some artists evolve with the people by expressing their connectivity and willingness to change.

Among those who arrive at many art forms, with music being the platform, Bob Marley and the Rasta nation's energy advocates for one-love. Producers of music such as Quincy Jones, who evolved his energy from *It's My Party*, *Thriller*, to speaking on a political platform promoting global world peace, love, and happiness—artists create the sound emitting the vernacular of our souls.

"Not one drop of my self-worth depends on your acceptance of me…"

-Quincy Jones

Art is embedded in us—it's why we buy the shit. Love in motion is the visual connection we see as humans coming together as individuals in a venue during a performance.

Taylor Swift created music as a bridge for many people to cry rivers over and drown out their momentary sorrows. She also made a song I twice partied to. And because I once dreamt with a broken heart, I created a bridge with John Mayer's guitar and acoustic creations.

My father thought I'd end up in the picture hip-hop and rap paints for the world…but he was wrong. If he were here today, I'd tell him I don't get to be in those pictures—I'm here to appreciate it. The communities that support it, for the artists to thrive, paint that picture.

Most of us are here to watch, respectfully.

Music, whether a picture in your head, an era you recall, or an imminent emotion, brings people together for our understanding… It's made for our energies to be in motion; you can see it move when the music comes on. Hence, *E…motion.*

Emotion is the abstracted energy we embrace or instead embraces us. From good emotions, sad emotions, to our angered feelings, these emotions are genuine to every listener. Rhythm puts distinct meanings behind it. And what's great about it, is you can decide that emotion.

I'd argue that if you don't understand or appreciate a particular genre of music, then you don't care to understand the origins of the people who created it. And to a degree, its purpose. The artist, who emerges from the people, creates the music. So maybe you don't want to embrace the genre's culture, either…

Music makes possible this allusion of love amongst others at a concert—where the sounds enable us to *love thy neighbor*s who are bumping into shoulders unwelcome. It's love in the allusion that a genre's supporting audience enables respect to its people and listeners—to empower the awareness for their communities to thrive. It brings an understanding to people through the artists' lyrics—which is why we greatly appreciate them as beacons of the world…they are the voice of the people.

And lastly, about love you reading jive-turkeys… the allusion music creates is the structure for our lives—because everyone has songs or a playlist for moods that sets the tone for what we want to do. For me, music grants the grace as a function to thrive, empowering people to organize and focus on loving, laughing, and fun stuff to where no one's getting hurt…

Music takes listeners beyond understanding, beyond meaning, and into a perception where we're connected to the artist. We appreciate their stories as if it's our soundtrack we're partying to.

If it feels good, you'll move better. If you're moving better, you'll be better. And if you're *being* better, you'll create better—not art specifically, but again, more fun stuff.

∞

COINED AT THE OREGON SYMPHONY WHILE EXPERIENCING TCHAIKOVSKY V. DRAKE, THIS IS MY LIFE STORY TOLD THROUGH SONG LYRICS WITH POETIC RUCKUS. FIND YOUR FAVORITE LINE AND MAYBE I'LL SHARE THE STORY BEHIND IT… BUT FIRST, THANK THE ARTISTS—WHO BRING OUR STORIES TO LIGHT. THEIR WORDS AND ART IS AN EXPRESSION OF THEIR PEOPLE, AND THEIR PEOPLE ARE YOU!

Budd's Soundtrack: Volume II

December 12, 2018

No pop, no style, I'm strictly words—majority truth.

Mistakenly a cocky son of the dead rich. And with no will over his dead body, I cry up hilltops of glory, telling stories since Bone Thugs N' Harmony.

And so, these songs finally have resonance with me, and not just hopeful pipe dreams, but a vocal beast who cares for me.

Coming to Fruition a bit early, and overstanding why the Sun shines with you, it wouldn't be until after I cried over his dead body that I'd fill an ocean blue thus widely.

Before I got caught up in girls, girls, and more girls' worlds, I wandered about heaven's ghetto in diamonds and pearls.

Crazy girl, you know that I loved you. It took gallons of tears to become fool proof from you. You made my days blue, and that's the best I got from you…

Because Blue is my color. Blue is my throne. Blue is my home, the one my father and I had lived and grown. Now, another Blue ranch house they say I'll fiduciarily own. Much further than Dekum's home; down below the Hilltop of glory's dome.

So if they wanna' know what was going on in the South, Blue's also my kinfolk's lake house.

You woulda' thought we come from Trench Town, freeing the people through music. But we come from Portland, Oregon—#amwriting to free people of anxiety and stupidity's amusement.

Baton Rouge's roots sent me. My dad's dad was heaven's devil so excuse me if I'm aloof, shit…

After all, Umi did remind me to shine my light on the world. Shine it on those who feel today couldn't have been the best day ever.

But who woulda' thought it'd grow from the scary days on my concrete floored apartment? I'm now the flower who once couldn't learn as my mind spent bent.

Through an evident War With God, I learned to breathe. I first couldn't breathe without you, but I had to. Later accepting that people are people and sometimes it doesn't work out.

But today, I make me proud. American Dreamin', Can I Live?

Let a nigga live….

…to reminisce the days off Ol' English, Black Panthers, Illuminati, Free Masons, and now a freelancer, better yet, world enhancer.

Don't blink twice this is an uptown society. I'm often cocky with a subtle mental capacity. There, can you read me?

Anyways, I had an excellent father, and his strength didn't make me stronger until he died. Yeah, I cried over his dead body.

The tears evaporated off his shell, and I inhaled them to become untouchable, unstoppable, and undesirable if you get it. At the time our vibe wasn't right. This is top ranked writing. No corporate fighting.
I told leaders I'd be rising up yonder; but they ain't listen. Now I speak

broader as they laugh at subordinate emails by those bitchin'.

They'll hear me speak on accident murderers—the sucka's of society. Making people cause a ruckus, what's wrong with our policies? Regardless, they'll spin it to remind niggas we aren't heard entirely.

They'll ignore truth, because it's easier to admit to their own; learnt in their home.

In closing, I heard a few great men speak on the new album with Meek.

Because most of us are truly ignorant of a plan. Ignorant of world demand.

Don't mistake this for GOD's plan. Your attention. Which is often spent from command. Now you have a man dangerous, relentless, and saying fuck you ☺

Label me how you feel, it's often mis-scanned.

And when you meet me, I'll welcome you to the good life—summa' time Chi….

That's free. Thanks, me.

So go and strut your white collar. Wipe the blue collar you claim. I write to avoid fame. Most influencers calling the kettle black—underwhelmingly lame.

Ya'll see that fancy Alto Saxophone? Well, last week it was delivered to my home. Another art form for the people, a culture overworked under a made up throne by an earlier creature outgrown.

∞

Ain't It A Vibe?

February 12, 2019

And about an artist's written work; between the producers, performers, and song writers, there transcends a synergy of high emotion. From sad, mad, chill, excitement, glory and a true toe tapper, we humans emit vibes at the sound of music.

It can feel so beautiful, but you must agree…

And when you do, think what images come to mind when you hear a certain genre of music. For example, rap, country, rock, alternative, R&B, pop or KIDZ BOP.

It's a difficult image or thought to project on the spot. Most genres are generational and have subtypes.

But about art—it's a finite expression of the human's highest attained frequency. From emotions, memories, sensations and all that good stuff, art makes life sexy.

An artist's journey, from their first playing note to ending chords, draws an emotional frequency that people only experience when creative waves match amongst each contributing artist. By each of them sharing thoughts, words and emotions, it results in what illustrates love out the creatives' compassion.

The heart is then understood when appreciation is reciprocated.

Although energies must consistently match for the art to be relevant, relevance in itself is based on the viewers, listeners, and those who experience the art, past experiences.

You wouldn't understand a country artist's song never having embraced his/her experience, or could you? A rapper's lyrics—it wouldn't resonate with you if you've ignored their communities, culture, and history, right?
But back to music.

Rap and country are only two examples. Art is subjective to the creator's resonance, and where they decide to direct it, is up to their frequencies held en route to creating the finite piece of art—like a painting, song, poem, dance, book or whatever odd shit a creative creates.

What I think is most important, is the people they envision attracting to their finished work. This has nothing to do with 'law of attraction', but all creatives who pursue progressive action, then later find out their art isn't catching. Who's to blame?

An artist isn't themselves without the experiences of a culture in contrast. So the trio of creatives don't work well without this synergy of happenings. From each creative contributor first expressing their disagreements with each other, then discussing if it's worthwhile, and boom, they find that their vibes are dominated by one color.

Although money may rhyme with that hue, their words don't. #IssaVibe…

∞

Budd's Soundtrack: Volume III

March 24, 2019

#AMWriting back to my sax, read the pudding, it's in my facts.
The untouchable negro you regret to ask,
Writing the music to later produce with my sax.
They must've got it wrong bout' TKane bruh…
He wasn't writing this crap, but like the W4 you signed,
This is my modern day slavery trap.
No jewelry from this land on this man,
Only the countries of oath.
I love you all, though,
I come with an addiction; a word and verbplay conviction.
If you see me, write a toast!
A poet's W4; a personal tax.
Book one so far gave me a panic attack.
Imagine what's next with my fuckin' sax.
Through sound we can tell the energy's black.
So, let me know.
From the time I was broke, to when I can pull up in my Mfoe.
Running with trouble left and right, be still fucka's I run to write.
You're reading a free man, a loved man.
A BMW driving black Man.
A Black Man Winning in Life, damn.
A Black Man Writing his future; watch my glam.
Now your eyes stuck, I know when you're star-struck.
A Black Man Who's wage's close to Scrooge McDuck.
I'm not a rapper, people, but an imposter writing wordplay and poetry deeper.
On the run and writing to funds.
Driving to runs; at Tom McCall Waterfront to sing to the people on my tired stretches of the run.
Crossing our Tilikum, running beside the max killin' em'…
And here's my watcher's oath.
First beacon under the equator.

A Muse In Tunes

Sweating to Rigil, body of lies so braver.
Better to please her.
#AmWriting back to your Pink Panther.
Red Rocket where the scary man was.
Watchers know well, not those selling out to protect and dwell.
But driving to dreams.
#AMWriting back to Brooklyn.
First-class to show up with my Book One.
Just watch, I'll blow my saxophone soon.
I'll play to the Booj-Wah-Zee tunes.
Last, let me tell you about Las Vegas.
It's a player's playground; I've been up there but first, down.
It was GoDucks baby; this negro been around the real late spree.
Drinking out the bottles, with girls who just stalk dumb.
For the gram' and stunt.
Bitches. I don't tip her, but fuck the best of her.
I know a pimper's fur.
If you don't know me by now, let me entertain you; I'm a magician.
Was that Budd they talmbout' driven?
Star risen?
Inspired much before Dekum's Blue?
Yep. Here I am to read you.

∞

Respect The Fighting Journey

(NIPSEY HUSSLE DEDICATION)

April 1, 2019

If one could teach the world, he'll bring others to the free world.
Mothers to reach a world, and Fathers to teach their girls.
Like hate, it's in respect and the other's confused trust.
Yet trust will be at the others' cuff.
Secrets that stars expose in fighting.
Behind the scenes dividing…
Words for the confused, it often seems inviting.
The attention brings you into their journey.
Life after suicide, not many can respect I'm never returning.
Reaching others in ways the haters can't see,
but must we be put into a coffin?
The pillars of this world speak often.
Stars don't shine on each other.
They teach to reach one another.
Pretend to meet with one another.
The respect's in the unseen meaning for shining together.
It's what happens when a star shines out the gutter.
Through darkness even in light, they'll shine forever above your utter.
A dreamer's test, why put him to rest?
The doer's mess, likely believing his best.
You decide.
This is wordplay, not necessarily for people to confide.
In us shining forever in Dekum's Blue.
Rapping to forever inspire you.
Psycho now, too…
I'm black; I'm always afraid who gone' shoot.
#AMWriting to be protected by love.
#AMWriting to inspire those above.
I live in harmony.
No medication for love, but trusting this writing's beloved.

Respecting a forever continuing journey.
A rapper fighting forever, so yes, we can continue in glory…
Writing this letter from the king.
Our hearts out to his family.
Irrelevant to ask, but why at 33?
Is this history repeating things?
Now we know what it's like to be a thug in many harmonies.
Hater of one, bringing sadness with what he's done.
Young and dreaming, but again, we continue despite the killing of another great being.

∞

Memoirs With A Fighter (Part One)

June 16, 2019

For the songbird he became, Sundays at this moment, my father would sing to the congregation. Meanwhile, his son[me] sitting four pews back not caring for the hymn, was in trance daydreaming a new one.

As he began preaching, I'd daydream imaginary flights to just about anywhere around the world, awaiting his, "…and in closing," statement because after that it was like the final approach before wheels down, and we got to drive home.

As those dreams came home with me, I'd play them out with my toys. It was also our layover, because he'd require us to go back to church for another flight segment. I mean, evening worship.

Maybe I ignored my father's sermons too much. But it doesn't matter, I took home what he meant to give the people listening.

I've traveled enough to forecast lost baggage. And most of us don't check luggage anyway, afraid the airline would lose it—it's also getting expensive.

My father never heard my dreams, because he was more concerned about me showing up to church on time, forever. The older I got, the more reluctant I was to tell anyone about the dreams I had in church. The same Budd riding to the airport, was the same Budd who tried to build an airplane in our backyard with the Honda lawnmower. He saw the mess, and destroyed the wooden wings I began with.

Asshole.

But the lawn would've never been cut; what the hell was I thinking at seven?

My dad last smiled two days after I met her, then he passed on. So, to clear things up, I can't prove to his generation I'm not gay because I didn't marry in my 20's… But I'd tell him, like the people I do this for, they too misread me. TheWriter is for the people to stop assuming of me. My dreams, like hers, take off from 28L—giving both the heavens and hell something new to spell.

Now in closing, #AmWriting this as a token of reclaiming. Imagine church just ended, we're thanking the pilot, I mean preacher[him], and soon heading home for either a Sunday layover, or to settle with our toys on vacation. The reason I often didn't want to return to evening worship, was because I was home with my luggage. That is, his voice.

∞

Memoirs With A Fighter (Part Two)

June 16, 2019

Some glad morning,
when this life is over,
I'll fly away.
One long mourning,
looking up to Dekum's blue,
grateful he flew to stay.
If heaven be his space,
maybe I'll breathe til' it's in my face.
There's something about full moons,
Like when he spoke,
It was white-noise that bloomed.
I still hear the songbird sweeping away,
Even if he never picked up a broom anyway.
Yeah, he never cleaned,
But Sunday mornings he did so repenting.
When I tried sharing with him my last dream,
He smiled and remained sleeping.
From the fighting preacher,
To his son's readers.
I wrote this hungover.
Still able to get a message sent over.
Like the singing fighter in church I watched,
It's Summertime, dad, and from above watch a partying writer in flight.
Who won't lose luggage,
Because the experience is how Budd flies this.
Flying with love, writing through trust.
The colors you sang, inspired us much…

∞

What Summer Should Write Like

July 17, 2019

Writing back to the summers of hell.
Writing back for the summers I failed.
Booking flights taking off from 28 L.
Looking back for a sun to prevail.
Because my daddy isn't here.
Most of ours aren't, and no one cares.
It's hot enough to cry.
Okay, so mines died.
With that I built my own well.
And ran Portland, singing for the pale.
They get scared of the anxiety I detail.
Writing to home so the blue is my following trail.
Blazing each scenery.
Shining on our greenery.
Danger's in the repeating tree.
Try something new next sun.
You'll love the times we had no funds.

∞

Proofs In The Mail

July 19, 2019

Mr. Postman, where art thou?
My book's in your hands, and now.
From Amazon's 1-day shipping,
To me, a letter of the dream; am I tripping?
Still at the facility, huh?
The waiting's tough, bruh.
The writing's even more rough, because;
Day by day I wished to give up.
So, you withhold a dream.
Deliver it faster.
The sooner the better.
278 pages; with words of a master.
Am not re-writing a song.
But for a book to better a wrong.
Proof's in the mail.
Wrote thoughts to unthink and prevail.
Out the gutters or assumed hell.
Here we are; soon in a box of pars.
Fitted truly for who we are.
Writing by night the scars.
Rhyming; but am not a rapper with bars.
Yet a negro writing who I truly are.
Reflecting my flesh.
Running to meet you.
Under stress I deliver best.
Poetic walker, and synced talker.
What's all this mean?
From Portland **I write in between**.
Now awaiting a book fixing colors we see.
Reaction to the masses of the unforeseen.
Historical content as my thoughts breathe.
Thank you for reading.
Now off to speak as I once did dreaming.

∞

What Are You Drinking Tonight?

September 16, 2019

Bourbon of Kentucky how so you do?
4 bottles later and look what I flew.
Not a plane but many words.
And verbs I stewed.
Summer disturbed.
Who woulda'…
Knew..!
Each story's legit.
Now a connoisseur with it.
No driving for there's a price.
And everything to do with it—DUI.
Dimwit… the former me also the ignorance of free.
Writing from below concrete feelings to words I spree.
Coming down to harvest faith each step, and a promise you kept!
Half gone but the work's sublime—no money but that's fine.
The meaning in dollars will come after self is described.
Bold and old, 32 years told, now my past I scold.
Better yet lessons untold, as failures unfold.
To be honest, I love this person I behold.
Not everyone understands me.
It's a blessing to hold.
Painful to mold.
I get it, though.
Dreams are…
Tough!
Most will,
Give up
But you, Bourbon.
I've drank plenty of you.
Ice cubed in my glass cups.

∞

Take It And Let Go In Faith

November 3, 2019

Waking up without it, it bleeds away overnight. It's there before sleep arrives, but carries no trust to stay. In the morning I must chant for it, call out the names, and remind all watchers of their purpose. They too sleep—in the cold airs of the dark as if the matter lay their bed.

It arrives at some point stronger than ever. With a breath comes the gut punch, and a good feeling to watch for. Your response is never important, just do what breaths do, and let go. It'll make its exit soon, so take it with gratitude. And again, let go.

It'll keep happiness in a high place, but do not identify with it. For you have it, therefore awareness is all which is required. It completes the now, confirms the afore, and says the future is just one step ahead.

Just take it, and let go.

∞

Lions Don't Lie

November 8, 2019

Create a space so the mood can open.
#AmWriting to people I hope to rope in,
To dreams I once deserved.
It's what I must stand to earn.
We are people who make the future.
We are creatures who remember the past.
Some connecting for an everlasting grasp,
Onto others and our love outlasts,
The pains of whom we may laugh.
Navigate to the top for a victim to be inspired.
…from there a survivor must be transpired.
But never forget who propelled you aspired.
It's those looking up to say,
"We helped you, so don't give up, okay…?"
Otherwise they'll deem you expired.
What's worse, a tree on fire?
Or a lion'd up liar?

∞

#AMRunning With Music To Write

November 9, 2019

It wouldn't be enough to visit a landmark, take a picture for Instagram, and share with the world I'm there. Fulfillment isn't in showcasing my traveling ability to appreciate beautiful places, statues, or infrastructures, but it's something else…

Traveling is an affirmation for the soul; we are meant to seek new places of old creations and become the allowing self who experiences the journey.

A selfie is proof, so what constitutes your checking for who cares?

Some of us travel to be looked up to, others explore to venture into new cultures and see what in the world our world is oblivious to. We can be nosy creatures, and live to say, "this landmark looks more beautiful with me in it…"

I took the feature photo before running along the Santa Monica Pier, just hours after the 2016 Los Angeles WordCamp. The song which marked it a memorable run, "Hold On" by *Alabama Shakes*, ran me crazy.

What is it about a song that takes us to places we aren't at? Our living rooms become the night club, the gym becomes a warrior training facility, because the music on this run turned the Santa Monica Pier into the stage of my first air-saxophone performance.

Hold on a bit longer, I'll be back. To run a beach and dance to places music allows me to be at. Maybe the music is the landmark?

Forever existing in a place music invites me to thrive…

∞

Can You Fly Out Of Love?

November 15, 2019

The answer is as mysterious as time.
Where does it come from—where does it go?
Does time have a name?
Maybe it's the heartbeat one after another?
If lucky, it's beating next to the one you call your lover.
Spending time together, it beats much better.
Spending your lives together, it's greater.
It feels like it beats forever.
But where do those previous heartbeats go?
Where do the future ones come from though?
Maybe an airplane flying around and under our nose…?
We can't see it, it's like love just takes off and goes…
Through the wind as it kisses and blows…
Saying, "hi," and "goodbye," from eternal windows.
Why must you tease?
My heart needs a partner to grow.
I'll share it for now and alone my hope knows,
…even love forever is temporary if clever.
Does love have an On & Off button?
Show me to the lever.

∞

Because I Questioned The Morning Dew

November 26, 2019

How would you explain the ocean to a fish?
What's the cost of living inside the box forever?
Who benefits from living beside the river?
Are there angels flying above volcanic ground?
Do we really understand animal's communication methods?
Whats money got to do with your next breath?
Are near death experiences there to teach us?
Why do you want to look so confident?
Does awkward paint the picture for new information, but in fear?
Some people can't handle *truth*, but who cares?
The awareness of life is just—now what?
Are some words taboo only in context?
If you don't build context, some things don't make sense, right?
How specific must we get to capture attention?
The sky falls every year, month, day, oh wait, it's not falling, it's just…
Does happiness exist? Or, is it only a word? Because I feel fine.
How about you?

∞

I QUESTIONED MYSELF THE OTHER DAY, ABOUT THE WORDS I FIND MYSELF WRITING. I SHOW MY EMOTIONS TOO MUCH, WRITE FROM TOO DEEP OF A SPEAKING GUT, AND MY HEART IS WRITTEN OVER AND OVER DAILY. BECAUSE OF THIS WRITING HABIT, IT'S PRESENTED ME A GIFT—A NEW FRIEND TO REMIND ME OF THE EVERLASTING GIFT. WHAT IS LIFE? FOR NOW, THINK OF IT AS THE APPRECIATION OF THIS NEXT BREATH YOU TAKE.

…..SO DID YOU TAKE THE BREATH YET?

Do Your Thanksgiving In The Next Breath

November 27, 2019

This is my gift.
This is my loving gift.
My gift to me.
My gift to you.
My gift to life.
I wake up.
Mind says what what what am I?
Mind has so many questions.
My heart has 1 answer.
I stretch.
I flex.
I run.
I breathe, see, feel, sense & witness.
I am just this.
Every bit of what I witness.
Letting me be this gift.
I am just this being.
And then arising for my being.
This is my loving gift.
I am this loving gift.

∞

Never Not Look Up For You're An Angel

December 3, 2019

I'm not enough for my greatest being's gifts.
The people would rather wish me well, than help me prevail.
The desire to succeed is the bullet to my foot.
I ask self, "are we happy lonely?"
Is dog soft enough; for the holiday nights we get cozy…
No one hears my cries.
I know I am not that.
It's how deep my emotions spell.
I know I am not that.
A hole in the world—almonds for autocorrect did that.
A dream it breathes abundantly around me.
A dream for it streams walking beneath my feet.
A dream for I can smell it as we eat.
A dream for the touch is on repeat.
A dream for flutes eases my thoughts of you.
Faith in a dream I see but yet to you.
I think flow; for the steaks are soft and tender for chew.
I hurt but it's not my view.
I wrote a book to inspire today's you.
You are not your pain.
Look up a new angel awaits you.
You must first breathe and turn to page two.

∞

Can A Train Of Thoughts Create A Smile?

December 8, 2019

This is the color I become when needing to succeed.
The color I woke up in I trust was fair—I believe.
Colors are vibrations like the emotions we seek.
The color I am is not the same when weak.
A mellow mood for the others who assume I'm rude.
My dog watches the bums like she would any other DUDE.
Our vibrations have a color we can't see.
If I could teach the world, I'd allow my colors to blind the sky—
then breathe.
Because it isn't blue; nor is the sun yellow you foo'…
It's all subjective, contextual and relative.
My love is protective.
A meaning for the respective.
First 44 and missing a 4.
An angel I patiently wait for.
The color of love has no hue.
It's the smile you submerge beneath you.
Waiting to be one with you.
Here it is via emoji if words don't do it for you…
At least I answered a thought I first couldn't prove to you.

∞

God's Mann

December 11, 2019

From my very own Godtober of a month, I'll laugh in a year.
I did this without fear—but an illusion of sheer.
Listening to God's Plan to write the man,
My thoughts are God's plan so my heart stands.
I look within for his demand.
Call it fate, but better now as never is late.
I won't pretend anymore.
God's plan was for my wish to explore.
The stars I poke at.
The car I drive in black.
From the crash, it became my vehicle,
...of words I'll forever digest.
Writing in the chaos to confess.
Needing the works for a dream to protect.
I didn't plan this.
He showed me bliss.
God's plan?
Or, a man saving his land?
Either way gratitude's my new attitude.
Showing me my new life and spiritual altitude.

∞

A Message From Behind The Stars

December 15, 2019

What is this place? The flute sends its touch from a retro wave. Questions delay a process as sounds are creating the space.

Atop still waters can we unite? Ponder there as warm air travels between argon? The hurt was yesteryear, the suffering is still; but a guardian eagle soars above in peace.

So calm—as the other four moods await their turn. Care to explain such a state?

A walk through water. Swimming in the fire. Climbing the gases of ether. Take a bow for you did not explain—but rather the hills of this land express you.

Fear was the propeller. Right eyes, right time. Because we are enough. We are just. Beauty.

It becomes relative down there. Here it is, everywhere and forever. Pain is obliviated. Don't talk about it, we might go back. When the lad asks for help, revisit in context. They need to know where you truly were.

Not enough believe. Enough will always. It doesn't go anywhere. You do.

∞

A Swifty BuddDay

December 15, 2019

How did the number 13 become my lucky number? And because I'll be 33 years old this week, I pray Jesus takes my wheel. Three days prior to my 30th birthday, I crashed my BMW driving in the ice and snow.

The following morning, my father passed. Jesus took his wheel. Maybe I tried too hard steering mines.

In 2016, there were 13 months—don't believe me? Well, neither a reader nor myself can prove this. Don't show me the Pope's calendar; numbers are why we're here.

I give up in well-being because it's often not my decision. Jesus takes my wheel.

There's a bright and beautiful moon to my right. No one resides up there but I meditated looking straight at heaven's night lamp.

Who or what drove you here? Me? I have four uncles and nine aunts. My grandma' was the first beast I met. She birthed 13 of them. One passed shortly after birth. Jesus had her wheel all along.

Did you do this to the moon, Grandma'? It's still shining on me! Jesus must have your wheel.

In high school, kids told me I was random. It's what's writing this. Jesus must have my wheel…

And about Taylor Swift… I wrote my first suicidal letters on her 20th birthday. A lot has happened in ten years, including becoming happy.

I don't take it lightly, but when you come so far you learn to laugh at the ways you once thought. I wrote, "I hate my life…," then noted, "Happy Birthday T-Swift!"

I'm fully aware how different I am. I think so much that I wrote my thoughts in a book and self-published it on Amazon.

After turning 13, I wanted to wear no. 13 in the NBA. That was 20 years ago from today.

Half of 20 is 10, and half of 10 is 5, which is how many days away the 13th is from the 18th—my birthday!

Not only am I writing random for the sake of someone's birthday, but because of 13.

I ran 13 miles because it was in me. And so are these words which aim for readers to donate to my GoFundMe…

∞

A Poem For The People

December 18, 2019

You all are so beautiful.
The words to describe are chanting.
What water brings is solely your voice.
How we interpret things; so be it our choice.
I chose nothing today.
But here I find myself to say.
If you hold two pupils above your nose,
...below the instrument to say what flows.
Why life separates us by things we don't see?
I don't answer, but enjoy the scenery.
A poet who turns 33.
A gift which doubted at 23.
Ten years in the making, happiness craved me.
One question I can answer.
The people are my gift I only write to see.

∞

Uncle Sego Inspired

December 19, 2019

By a random playlist of his I write to, and so many terminals to fly you, which
flight should I type to? Which notes should I blow through?
Starting fresh, I lose thoughts and await an order of words to stress.
I too have a vision; a wall full of those who inspired me. I'm also writing a wall
full of those who transcended me.
Lady Lady, she took off for the Navy.
Open mic I'll bring my creativity.
How and when? I can't tell you, just trust in me.
How I got here? Don't know.
Looking back, I may not grow.
My walk of faith could include you though.
We are where we're meant to be due.
I'll fly across the Atlantic to bring my profound sights and views.
Don't doubt me—if I told you how I'll succeed,
Might not make it there to see.
Hell, I don't even know.
I breathe, blow, and go.
I believe, then grow, and to my readers I owe,
My vision.
Seeing their eyes in precision.
I don't see my next step—
am not trippin'…
There's a voice in me saying, "just walk boy…"
Therefore, I proceed through this mission.
Bringing my sax to compose the sound.
I'll show up like TADOW…
Thank you and goodbye for now.

∞

A Poetic Goodnight Into The New Year

January 1, 2020

Flickering each string, a tune ignites their moves.
Take two steps per motion, ease into the grooves.
Can you hear the flute?
The sounds are beautiful like you.
What are sounds without roots?
The vibes hit us through waves; welcome to *Jamuary*.
You feel that?
The music's throwing vibes—get jiggy.
Got no rhythm?
No biggy.
What you did coming into the new year,
Do it all year when facing a fear.
Dance with them, sing along with them.
Do what got you here and smile with friends.
It's a new world out there if you want to.
Create the next new great thing.
It can be as simple as breathing.
Don't believe me?
Don't watch.
Goodnight.

∞

Next To An Ember Mug

January 2, 2020

Who else almost writes 2019?
Is it too early?
We can still mess up and get away with it…?
I think I have a crush on the weather lady.
How would I know it's real?
I have a hard time at the grocery store.
But I must go.
I'm editing a book.
Started back on my birthday in 2018.
I was due on Christmas Day of 1986.
I ran through the new year.
Running into New Year's Day.
There I went to see him grow.
It was dark and cold, but I was running to gold.
Like a jungle and the path unfolds.
My safety lights shine, flash, and glow.
Freedom runner and to the tunes I blow.
Singing and breathing.
Wild child of the Newbirth repeating.
Words everlasting to practice a spoken thing.
One to echo beautiful wordings,
…for those who create endless endings.

∞

#NOWPLAYING: My Playlist To Writing Book One

January 9, 2020

I'm a maniac writing crazy for cash. I miss my grandma'—she raised the beast in me. The saxophone inspires me. Whether I'm writing a cover letter, resume, email, poem, journaling, editing a book or texting, I'm writing into the future.

And so are you.

If I could teach the world anything, it wouldn't start with how to be a thug in harmony, rather how to stay yourself in society. First, assume you are the world's greatest in your next task, and tell no one.

It's a great song. Despite the man's ugly past, there's a feeling you can't deny the song provides. Allow me to prove it.

The hilltop down the street from my home was once dreadful to run. Last time I ran the hill I made it my bitch. Took a right turn at the top as it continues up, and with no side-roads I danced and sang my way further up.

Altitude, no issues. I ran up to Lord Knows—because it's in God's Plan to help me remember those songs.

I may look skinnier, but like Damo once told me, "you gotta' go higher each time." This made my muscles defined.

Failure got me going higher, it keeps on liftin' me up inspired—to inspire. It's what trusting does to me. Now to you I transpire.

There's a reason these words rhyme with fire…

Leaving the rivers to dissipate, feel weary yet? Source must be cloudy? With the securities you lost, it's leading to the wars in your head, seeking your old sense of control.

Well, that was the river, and this is the sea…

BREATHE!

Shifting gears here, I just wanna' show you something a little different. And by writing from retro places, it explains who the hell Mr. Hansen is. As an alternative, his ego is all I have.

"Show me the green light!" He whispers as I awaken.

Some people don't get it. It's a brand-new part of me. It took a long, long time to get here. Many nights of crying for reasons I couldn't explain, but fear.

The greater disturbing cries distorted themselves into tears of joy. Through leaving the muddy waters alone, I was able to see it settle and flow to unite with waters across the new world. Soon, I found me in places I've yet traveled to.

Because I kept dreaming—it wasn't very hard. Except for feeling like no one was on my side.

I'm places I once dreamt to be. Looking back, I see my aggressive desire to control my dreams disturbed the settled waters—which is how things have been and will always be.

I blame me for those muddy waters. Accountability builds trust, allowing waters to unite for an eternity.

Now that my sentences are burning like gasoline, and spewing words as they're frolicking, recognize I am not a rapper. But soon a poetry slam dabber. To prove to you all I'm a hypocrite, this is what it's like to give it all you got tonight. This moment is all we have. How are you choosing to enjoy it?

Thank you for choosing to read my random creative writing prompt.

From the wyld-child creating, uptown top ranked writing businessman thriving, he's making all this shit up. Learning how his mind fucks with his emotional expectations.

In conclusion, my weather lady crush continues. I'll send her ***my book***.

If you want a simple takeaway from this chaotic lyrical wordplay thing, understand the five love languages. I wrote about mine's here. (THANKS FOR READING)

While writing these words, I can't describe my muddy thoughts, because they're written from the fire of music. And songs which transpired into imaginary stories. The writer in me was touched by the vibes of these songwriters and artists.

Although it's not my preferred love language, receiving gifts from people I've never met is rare and extraordinary.

But how random is it that these 70ish songs, from 7 different genres, come together and help develop a book? Maybe as random as the thought that I believe we all have a hidden playlist only listened to with headphones.

And a gift I won't hide is my heart—it's what these songs remind me to show.

∞

To The Good Morning We Unite

February 9, 2020

Drawing through space with my body.
Flexibility for the muscles so lively.
Each twisting motion a signal to calm me.
Out to space for a calling I move so.
Inner feels—but it's like yoga I don't go.
It's great to be loose.
My energy of an inner muse.
Who knew the two beings.
Each side of my ribs now releasing.
Tension from the bullshit we dwell.
Often wringing out the pains of hell.
Aiding an almighty beast who talks insane.
But how the writings brew a thought train so well.
And Sunday's here we get to run without rain.
Protect what we see out of the profane.
Spiritually grow and rewards through findings.
Proving the body draws an ultimate kind of lottery.
To the ground I looked down.
Up from it I picked.
Within I get it.
Prosperity.
We win.
Peace,
Again.
∞

Words Of Light To A Distant Passing Star

March 18, 2020

I often want to float forever up with you.
But since you left I found peace beneath this blue.
The hue you forever float through.
Where our times together fly mute.
With you now a distant star watching me.
Your 'MainMan' making you proud—I miss you.
What an awkward relationship we had—now respect is due.
This is where my journey takes you.
From the rivers you showed me.
I rowed them until finding my peace.
Whether it be a sea of struggle.
A path still muddled.
I seek to proceed.
To show the inner me, of you, faith's deed.
A father to son creed.
Not precisely religious teachings…
But the public's reading.
Your world renowned through seeding.
Follow me, dad, I promise to impress my sisters.
Pay back and bless my mother.
Care for my brothers.
With nieces and nephews, I'm now their distant watcher.
It's you returning despite leaving 2016 bothered.
Sick of that waiting room?
Many are sick today, scared of what that virus will do.
Like you'd say in church, "and in closing…"
I'm just getting started.
Watch me create and write a world so startled.

∞

A Journey Which Doesn't Know How, Can Only...

May 4, 2020

There it rose above the horizon.
They stare and thunder roars uprising.
Their eyes to share as rainfalls surprising.
The cattle chew bare and grass proceeds them.
Goodnight from there returns a morning kiss.
Our distant love so young as time we miss.
Where art your faith to take it today?
Into a stirring of things by those unseen.
Laughter up yonder now serene.
A hand to grab I made it by dream.
Night and night emotions to fight.
Dwelling within to win and unite.
Envisions of how we all take flight.
A game to watch as many breathe in.
No shame to carry of my brothers by kin.
Hear true stories they'll all be tellin'...
From podiums of truth, some will yell it.
First, of how we failed them to win again.
Second, will be a feast of chickens.
Third's a world of verbs to elate.
May the fourth be waters of internal lakes.
With you my words often create.
Happiness I'm real, never a fake.
But faith has taken all my ways.
Unable to prove, somehow I grow.
Just watch me today,
I often don't know...
Journeying as if I only know so.

∞

Dream A Love They'll Never Take

May 18, 2020

How many of us live on to experience childhood dreams?
For those who have we each fear others telling us to go back to what we've done before, and dream.
You arrive at the lighthouse of love.
Lonesome we float upon the oceans of trust.
Carrying on the aches a heart suffers.
Letting go of a past the mind utters.
I meet you in serene destiny and see the eyes of eternity.
Your smile so light it emits joy.
Maybe our souls met at peace when I was a boy.
But separated at the trenches which life employs.
Traveling unprepared roads, swimming uncharted waters…
Here we are older and forever annoyed.
Closing each eye I envision this scene; where to eat, what movie to see, and how to enjoy such simple things.
I open each eye and realize my queen.
Still an experience of a young boy's dream.
But I win in the space because I don't look back.
I'd never let the doubters take our love as easy as that.

∞

If We Read Art In Its Colored Context

May 26, 2020

I promise you'll have enough dreams to choose from.
After every morning, reach for the awesome feeling…
So that you won't loose one.
It'll be in your karma to repurpose the ugly ones.
We're ordinary people dreaming an alternative life to veer from.
Act as you know, though you don't, so your imagination flows on.
Count to three, take a breath, and drive through the illusions of stress.
And face a fear, for the other side dreams come undone.
It's scary like a negro named Larry, but…
He'll be the one pissing his pants as courage outweighs weary, thus…
Forever going forth each fork in the road; dare me.
Anxieties of my past which got me here; bare with me.
Stories of the fool who dreams daily without rules; embarrassing.
A journey so rare but unto you I pray to share; join for free.
Stillness through the night and breathing mighty light; births new life.
Thinking overnight allowing visions to show what's right; there is a price.
A becoming of the black sheep; an insane repeat…
Of good things no one sees, and managing our negative peeps'.
For those who see, them who see when shown, and they who choose not to see, for I've repeated Leonardo Da Vinci.
An appreciation to a passing artist and a feature photo into this poetic read.
This concludes today's memorial of an artist,
An artist sharing an alternative humane dream.
And a reminder of how our colors misrepresent some things.

∞

Just Blew It

September 8, 2020

As the wind blows, so do I.
From a studio beneath these writing tries.
A note, B note, all three up top, G note.
Do this long enough I'll play into my bank account, C notes.
Sounds beautiful and you ain't gotta agree tho'…
Just watch post pandemic when I'm blowing easy flows.
From sax lessons at Tubman, & at the church teaching me said notes.
Blow it like I know it.
Amateur days, own it.
Squeaky sounds so soon profound.
From a corner near you as others drop their change—WOW!
Am not homeless just passion blessed—tadow!
Masego inspired and FKJ transpired.
What that means—these beasts are blowing machines.
Aiding a melody I had no idea how to string.
It sounds so clean and soon you'll agree.
How so? I'll blow so.
Like Kenny G, somehow I'll catch bro'…
Just as I did blowing random keys.
And in between writing words at ease.

∞

Body Of A Dancing Eye

September 26, 2020

Just Breathe Me,
And watch me.
Create me,
Just this one time, breathe.
How rad you see?
I'm amazing in me.
It's easy like free.
You were waiting, like, please,
I wanna see you dance with me.
Sway them hips with ease.
You can feel I've got a groove by the beat.
It's funky how I move my feet,
Catch em' if you can, that man's doing his dance.
Creatively partying a writer—shall we land,
Take that right foot; like that—bam!
Match it with them shoulders, damn!
Man of the year two-steppin' his jams.
In the dark so no one see's his glam.
Flex the empowerment—be a beast out it, man!
Don't gloat about it, grow about it.
Dekum's grown and that boy flew up out it.
Into outer space—what else is there to do without it?
End up right back into you, thinking doubts out loudly?
Might as well breathe a new body.
Make that negro dance so proudly.
Can't fool these eyes which watch me.
They're what I embody.
Breathe me, and watch me party.

∞

Inspired Through Smiles Of Pure Imagination

January 23, 2021

Whoever told you that one day you'd become a superstar, you better have taken the inch and ran a mile…

For the suffering creatives, thriving artists, and future innovators who'll get this, be okay with the contrasting process of your finite creative journey.

When people learn you created each dimple beside your smile, you become a star, and this makes you smile even more. Soon you'll find yourself hiding it. Why? Well, you've seen your smile well enough behind closed doors. And that's my best guess…

It's okay to reserve yourself and your passions—for everything you're preserving it for. So do that…

Anyways, while each dimple's hidden behind your skin of kin, you paint the hidden smiles, draw the forbidden sorrows, and then sell it. Because artists gotta' make money too…

So hustle your passion—give it all your energy and do that tonight!

And after you smile, let it go to allow the next to show.

But always remember, those who create smiles aren't often doing so. Although the smile will eventually glow, in the act of creating, visions instead must flow. Most of the time it's not fun.

From body to mind, mind to hand, and when the hand transcribes onto paper, the face sits still so the canvas won't croak. Before that surface of nothing turns to something, it sees your smile's oath. Sometimes that nothing exposes itself as tears of pain, or the illusion that we're nothing.

If you don't understand what I'm talking about, here's the take way. The process between something being insignificant and that something becoming significant, is a bunch of nothingness. It's where people are confused, get hurt and give up.

Just trust the process. More importantly, respect it—because you are the process.

You're the superstar in the making. A superstar who's creating. And not just canvased art, but smiles for miles…

∞

Wake That Ass Up!

October 8, 2021

Soon, you'll do morning different,
That tea will sip splendid,
It's stirred, isn't it?
Drink slowly, it's hot!
Pair it with an apple, scone or what not…
Cinnabon for a sugary morning run,
Bun apple tea,
This morning's on me.
Words to end a week.
Verbs to move as we,
Bring a weekend to hang so free,
Cause we're jailed at work, good grief,
Yearning for the hour we leave,
Come home to a house in defeat.
But the weekend is here, finally.
Maybe coffee does it, not tea,
Either way, it's Friday, okay?
Maybe you WFH all day?
Thinking, freedom's a walk away,
My couch is right there,
Why wait?
That's right, we need a payday.
Rent's due and you can't be late.
Anyways, there're two days that wait,
Assuming you get through Friday,
But come Monday, don't worry,
A cup of coffee or tea awaits,
As soon as your lazy ass's awake

∞

I Like Country Music

October 13, 2021

I'm a nappy dread headed,

Hopeless romantic runner,

Poetic writing loner,

Boxing meditator,

Saxophone playing punk,

Japanese speaking weight lifter,

Who listens to all genres on Apple music—

Wondering who's more bothered? Me because I like country music? Or the individual who cringed after me telling them I can enjoy it?

There's a few toe-tapping jams I can run to. I've even gone as far and crazy to sing at the top of my lungs to many of today's greatest backroad hits.

This is why I find myself asking for her back when I know she's not good for me. But if loving her is wrong, then I don't want to be right. Maybe that's why she left.

It's hard getting over what you can't understand.

Maybe it's me. I'm a little bit harder to love than the rest.

SML…

That acronym means, Some Moments Last forever, but only if you got Budd in this b!tch. And no, I'm not talking about me being in this…

I smoke with life as if she's my wife. To be honest with you, I often take three to four months off from smoking [weed] to ensure I actually like the latest country music I've been bouncing my brains out to…

Okay?

So that's all I have to say, it's all I have today…

Kthanxbye ☺

∞

What If Tomorrow…

October 24, 2021

They email you for a Zoom call interview,
Or your crush texts you, "Hey you
..yes, you!"
What if our sky shows its blue,
after a Monday forecast of rain and morning dew.
Imagine that check arrives in the mail,
…despite several Mondays overdue.
Imagine your boss awards you, for being you.
And working hard to help your colleagues who often doubted you.
Do you ever envision coming home, and your spouse shows you dinner reservations?
They exclude the kids, too.
Hence the babysitter for a few,
So relax and be free.
You know surprises come in three.
So you could win the lottery.
Run into your idol or favorite celebrity.
Maybe finally get that car,
So you can go ahead and toss the metro card.
Actually keep it, every city ain't friendly to cars,
But if we're lucky enough to see a blue sky of invisible stars,
We can envision one asking, "You and I are closer than it seems we are,
…but nothing like these clouds, making you forget who you are."
What if tomorrow you become a megastar?
And it's you, asking you, "How far do you think we're apart?"
Don't dare try answering, be clever or smart.
Imagination's a *what if* game.
If you do it too much,
You'll look apart.

∞

Pest Control

November 13, 2021

These thoughts belong to you and only you when you say so or carry them out. Consider them like pop-up ads or pockets of memories from past successive moments, including a lineage of people and organisms. Most of these images, thoughts and transpiring emotions *can* continue to build over time without your permission. So, who are you?

You're a product of your past. You're also a product of what you think you should become. Think of yourself as a seed, or better yet, you're an evolved seed. Of course, today, you're a flower or yesterday's seed which has bloomed.

Seeds, so be it, are thoughts. The thoughts you water, nurture or feel optimistic about will guide you to your most optimal desires.

The caveat here is that these seeds don't know positive and negative. That's where you decide.

You must decide not to ruminate on the negative. More importantly, you must choose not to identify with the mind's negative thoughts, emotions, or images. They will always be there—and so will the positive. To identity means to carry out or act out with a narrative.

In every waking moment and breath, you must decide to follow through on the positive thoughts, as long as they do not harm anyone. Start by understanding time.

If you want to stop time, kiss someone worthwhile.

If you want to escape time, go and have a personal party while listening to your favorite music.

If you want to release time, inhale deep, then exhale and relax.

If you want to travel in time, read.

And lastly, if you want to feel time, shut up and write.

∞

BuddDay Wishes

December 21, 2021

To journey,
To live,
With earnings,
To give,
To share.
And until resting right here,
Yeah—there.

.

.

.

To see,
What we hear,
Enough to taste the joyous fear.
They don't teach this in schools.
Religions scold, ruled by fools.
That fool is also me,
Traveling to speak,
Voyages shared by an inner ME,
Because I felt it as I breathed,
It's the same air an airplane needs.

.

.

.

And how so you celebrate me?
Gagging tequila between dry heaves.
That ain't so sloppy—please.
I'm being the best of me.
A partying writer who enjoys the scene.
Of people in happy places,
Not mean.
I'm a poetic thinker,

Millennial being.
Reminding Gen Z,
I am not twenty-three.
But an 80's baby—you see…
'Nick at Nite' kid,
Who dreamed,
That by thirty-five,
Life's dance would also sing.

∞

My Father's Voice

January 12, 2022

A few years before my father passed away, he asked me two things; do I still believe in GOD, and why don't I go to church anymore? I grew up in a Christian household and attended church every Sunday. When I got to college, that stopped.

To be honest, I don't recall how I responded to my dad about GOD or church. At the time, I was experiencing neurotic thought patterns, in which some nights I'd pray to GOD that he does not wake me up. I'd also try suppressing a voice that's reminding me I'm a worthless black man who should drive himself off the nearest cliff.

Obviously, I never did, and it never got to the point where I was hospitalized. That voice, however, is the reason I once gave up church and the idea of GOD. I'd ask myself and this GOD we worshipped every Sunday, Tuesday, Wednesday, and sometimes Saturday, why would a faithful Christian be put through such mindful torment?

The answer never came until I convinced myself there is no GOD and then walked about this earth like an emotionless soul yearning for help. Ironically, that's when things took a turn for the better.

Although I was too depressed to apply for graduation and walk across the stage, I finished college, got a job, and established my needed structure. Some residues of that voice remained but only under certain emotional circumstances.

My life was much better at the time, so that voice was just a voice. Instead, I'd question that voice, asking, "So, what's your purpose now? Because today, I'm good."

My father studied the Bible, preached at church maybe once a month, and was a GOD-fearing man, dreaming I'd follow in his footsteps. All he knew was the Bible because that's what saved him.

Soon, I'll be able to share his story.

But for now, I think back to the day he asked me those two questions, and since then, my recollection has changed for reasons I don't understand.

What I do understand, is the voice that questions the voice—and that's the voice I followed once I got a grip on life. It's much more positive, progressive, and convincingly mimics the Bible's syntax.

Following through with that voice sometimes makes my writing come off biblical, GOD-like, or as if I'm trying to imitate writers of the Bible. But to be honest, that voice is naturally me. I often break down my poetry to simplify it for readers to not scare off anyone. The truth is, it's who I am, and I've decided not to hold back.

This journal is me writing that voice to show you how to shut up and remind you that a weak heart follows what cannot be questioned—whereas, what's questioned, fears unseen energy.

So as you read, make yourself aware of negative emotions. It's the energies that block the positive part of being human.

I once fell for one, and when I gave up, the other took over.

∞

Write Her By Sunset

February 15, 2022

She had to have walked in for a reason,
And so from there, she wrote,
Bout' a page I suppose.
I'm shy, I don't poke.
Maybe I'll write her in hope,
What could be but won't,
What I should speak but don't,
Who is she? I'm blown…
Earth's wildchild?
Model pro?
Main Character, I'd suppose—
Where our path's meet—that's dope.
Like a rom-com, but nope.
Face reality, c'mon bro.
Like sunsets, girls come, most go.
…I'll add one thing though,
She hid her eyes,
Like I know…
The sun's bright,
I liked her coat.
But fate peaks like most won't,
She couldn't hide her true glow.

∞

Travel P

February 20, 2022

P ain't for power if you got it.
Pivot, reroute it—never proceed how you started.
P ain't for protest—ya'll must've seen the reactive unrest.
Copy don't paste—reread and regroup, it's the proper humane pace.
P ain't for panic.
…no entity in this world pushing P for paper.
The P used to page her,
Broke his heart, cried al a carte, then hand wrote her a letter.
Feelings light as a feather, wishing we'll get back together.
But this P ain't for past, more like progress—dumbass.
P don't even practice,
The boy shows up and you bet he gets active.
P ain't got patience—time is now.
Although P can wait, never not present.
P ain't for pro, prep, or punk.
P never passed,
Flunk.
P flew miles for stamps,
His pages are cramped,
But P ain't for passport.
Dear Clinton Sparks, should I write more?
You see the P in her poise?
Found her pose on the wall,
Cost nothing to show this to ya'll,
But my property to write free for all,
Selfish tendencies but who else can I call?
Poetically writing so let me stop or I stall.

∞

Shut Up And Write

February 22, 2022

Write as if this is it. You're flowing out words in the dark. No one's going to edit this or read it. But if you want, have this be the raw style of word flow you plan to show the world. Do you have any intentions? This is typewriter fun. Ain't no going back. You write it. It's there for the world to see, if you want.

It could read as if a young boy was attempting his English and didn't learn grammar.

No pop, as in, no emphasis on the written paragraphs. These are simply words of you. No style, MLA, or APA. Just strictly roots. Seeded words from a collection of past moments. Isn't it beautiful how that all comes together, right now, over you?

Personally, I'm writing this on my way to Las Vegas, Nevada. And I'm not listening to Athena and Donna's 'Uptown Top Ranking' hit. I'm thinking of when I first flew, and my dad was next to me. We flew TWA into Shreveport, Louisiana, then drove to Jonesboro for a family reunion. TWA Flight 800 crashed the night before.

Anyways, do you feel your friends are waiting for you to do something spectacular? Maybe I did. But now I'm like, meh...

Looking back, there was no pop to it, no style. Just a flow of actions, rooted from a moment I once experienced by each thought of doing it. That was a hell of a dopamine rush.

At first, action is boring. Because action means shutting up and doing it. What's 'it'? The things you gotta' do to fulfill that dopamine rush—or satisfy your most absurd dreams and desires.

Rely on serotonin. That reliance can replace your cup of cortisol. Cortisol is a stress hormone.

Now, go list the first three things you'd have to do to pursue your most ambitious goals. Be sure to leave space between each item you list so you can describe the reasons you can't do them.

∞

My Way

February 26, 2022

Find balance in sharpening your tunnel vision. This is the level of focus you'll get better at through persistence. People will offer you advice, and if your gut doesn't like it, create a dialogue that begins with them explaining their intentions. However, your gut feeling is also what you must learn to understand—in that some advice is bitter and bones, and other advice is tender enough to melt in your mouth.

It'll nourish your body, improve your soul, and replenish the energies to progress on the journey you are choosing to take.

Doing something your way takes bravery. Courage is a great way to put it, too, but doing something out of peer joy is fun and rare.

Doing something out of imagination rather than memory is risky because our imaginations are just that, imagined.

Moving in your imagination, which in short is your very own trailblazing path, takes three concepts to live by.

First, you must establish the rules of your daily goals that build up to your monthly accomplishments, then annual goals. It's better said by establishing systems. This system will act as a defense, or a realm of protection—because others will challenge what they cannot see of you. People will attack it. This is when memory comes into play. You must learn the rules of your system—write them down to review each week.

Second, know when you're under attack and never overreact. Never lead with emotion, but rather, lead by the rule of kindness. Whether structured or malicious, criticism will come in many different forms. Forget your emotions and let them pass. Kindness, from there, must lead. It's best to start with a smile—it'll help redirect reactive energy.

Third, always remember where you started. Do not become so obsessed with a system that you forget who you once were. This creates a foundation of gratitude, appreciation, and compassion. Those who are watching already can see the change in you. Many who come from rags to riches, understanding they are one in a million, must also understand people who dwell in the rags, will only watch or dream of riches.

Your way may get you far and fast, but a valuable life comes from others seeing value out of you. Listen to those you trust—chew the meat, spit out the bones.

Be thankful. For when you succeed, you will have done it how you saw it, felt it, and wrote it.

∞

LÈS DOODIS

February 28, 2022

Life is a bike—because if you stop moving, you'll lose balance.

And so, you come at me with the kickstand argument. A motorbike and a bicycle can stand upright when the kickstand is out. If gusting wind doesn't, someone's gonna tip it over.

Ok—so let's say life's a dance, two-stepping, and we find most of you with two left feet. But it won't matter if you keep moving. You never know. Because hey, they even choreographed the crip-walk during the Super Bowl halftime show.

And I know you saw them foo's on their lowrider bikes during California Love?

But if life's a dance and you rode your bike to the juke-joint, what are you doing with those two left feet?

Get down?

Or get up?

If you do either, just remember, in order for you to get down you gotta get in deep!

So go on and be the smooth cat soaking up the dance wall with that Jheri curl. Or the country bumpkin smothering dirt all over the dance floor with his boots. Unless them boots are walking all over you, what's it to them gals hollering over for chew?

And don't worry, I didn't forget where I'm going with this, I just had to keep writing, or my bike would tip.

∞

Crack Co-Bliss

March 4, 2022

Warning: once you get there, there's no turning back. Turning back hurts. And unfortunately, those who do, end up in more harm than good.

To get there, you must stare long enough, so it unveils itself—that is, phosphenes, floaties, or those things crossing our eyesight that start mutating. It looks like a science class unfolding with each eye wide open.

And as we watch our inner-made petri dish do its stuff, the world happens. Stillness. Do it long enough, and you come to the fundamental nature of our universe. All you gotta do is stare for a long, long time.

Some people get there much easier by taking psychedelics, e.g., mushrooms, acid (LSD), sylvia, and cannabis *can* as well. But understand that those drugs are inhibitors.

They accelerate who we are, what we are, where we are, but not why we are. The 'how' is complex. The how and why is unveiled through a journey.

Storytellers, creators, and readers who care, if you stare long enough to reach what scientists refer to as the quantum field, you learn the nothingness of life. From there, you create, influence, and build structures.

We are just that, nothing. Once you accept that, this world is yours.

Now, shut up and try it—before it tries you.

∞

Bread Is The Child

March 9, 2022

When BOY is naïve.

For these are the days the sun rises to seedeth a boy. These days are the sunsets resting a boy of faith, for him to later carry a throne, share his own, and become a freedom writer.

When MAN is hurt.

Man, in the midst of his struggles, will not understand his journey. Man during pain only sees hurt. For his mechanisms of pattern recognition will act in dominance; therefore, pain will be of the future.

How WOMAN sees good.

Shall the man learn to shut up, the pattern dissolves. This dissolution brings the novel test of man's fate. That is, faith.

Now GIRL likes beast.

Man, like woman, feel memory, and hear what can be understood. Most *good* is rejected. When man awakens at the seed during pain and grows through his light of pain's divorce, he'll recall the days of hunger.

When WE are master.

Since pain no longer dominates, the good propels him. The purpose of recalling pain and hunger is *his* order, *her* light. Together, in this, is a dangerous and robust bond. This synergy threatens patterns of evil.

∞

Fly Out Tonight

March 14, 2022

Most people vacation and return home to the lifestyle, which is the reason for them needing a vacation.

We all must work. But in our wildest dreams, we desire a job that we can look forward to each day—where our colleagues celebrate us upon arrival to the office. Your preferred beverage awaits you at your desk, and you're constantly switching it up because sometimes life's a beach—even that gets boring.

After logging on to your computer, you have the option to get to work or go play because your occupation requires you to be in complete alignment with your well-being before progressing through tasks.

Discipline is emphasized in the job description. You can't just get paid to show up. But your daily objective is to ensure you've contacted the producer, your leader, or your boss—for lack of a better term.

Your boss is not strict. In fact, they don't care for your results—because as long as you connect daily, you're paid. The requirement of a satisfying connection is arbitrary. That fulfillment is determined on a day-to-day basis.

If you show friends or family members your job description, they'll think you're a part of a pyramid scheme, being taken for a cult, or it's bullshit—which to you it was at first.

What changed?

You took a leap in faith. You also became delusional, like a bodybuilder on day one who carried 25 to 30 percent body fat and got laughed at. After 60 days, those who laughed started to shout, "Okay, I see you!" Then, after six months, those same people began pointing, saying, "Man, I'm trying to get like you!"

So, remember, faith will guide you through perseverance. Perseverance builds character. That character turns delusion into reality. And believe it or not, soon, those who once laughed at your job description will be waiting for you to do one of two things; fail or invite them to join you.

Life is no vacation, but it's the longest 'thing' you'll ever experience.

∞

Dolce Far Niente

March 17, 2022

Sometimes I do nothing. I sit in my meditative pose either listening to music, journaling, or staring at the wall. I'm pretty good at it.

Sometimes I walk. Which used to be dog walks. Yeah I miss my puppy. But now my walks are meditative. My intention is to get closer to water.

Viewing water and as wet as it is, is like, WOW; because there's not much to it for it to be so calming and beautiful.

But a TV… turn that thing on and you're inviting a world of satellite pop-up ads. Or for some, it's simply the impulsive action of grabbing the phone.

So sometimes, I like to do nothing.

Fuck my phone.

Fuck the television.

∞

Love Her

March 21, 2022

Don't be surprised if you find her saying, "I told you so." She will also be the death of you if you fail to appreciate her, show her off, and care for her like your own child. There isn't much to react to when she turns her back on you for questioning her gut instinct. She's a wildflower, a firecracker, and it scares the hell out of you. But she's everything you asked for.

She'll be so good to you, like a caregiver, but she is not. She's no queen, either—for a queen needs attention and a flock to lead. She loves you because you're no king—for a king needs warriors, protectors, and a body of people to rule.

She—a wildflower—was planted in the ugliest environment. There, she awaited growth in silence and darkness amongst dirt, bugs, and earth's unseen territory. No one witnessed her first spout of change. No one watched her curdle in fear through darkness. No one heard her screaming for help as she cried tears of anguishing growth.

No, not one.

You may attempt to remind her of these episodes, but they have nothing to do with you. Assuming you can't sympathize, she'll quiet you and allow you to be on your way. If you can sympathize, she'll share with you her past pains in due time. In due time, she'll tell you what hurt really is. You must remember, she is not you. And your pains may only be relevant to hers by the words she chooses to share with you.

Life is forever moving forward. There is no reverse. For the reverse gear in a vehicle is there to position its tail to lead. It's the only time the rear leads. Assuming our past is the rear, we are often in reverse, following patterns of the many yesterday emotions.

She has moved on, and her vehicle has no reverse. Her past must be conjoined with yours—meaning, you two must experience a new path so that you trailblaze a new journey together. This new journey can now be looked back on by the two of you.

You wouldn't want to reminisce the journey you have taken together, only to realize you have been reflecting on each other's lives before meeting.

When her 'before you' arrives, let her cry—for she is a flower who dies through autumns, reincarnates to be seeded through winters, to bloom over springs into flourishing summers.

Therefore, you must let her die—or you will cry. You should avoid your tears being accompanied by her worst fear. She has no time for 'Mr. Me Too'. Not only will she have told you, but this, has written you so…

∞

We Can Love

March 26, 2022

Love is a weakness for those who do not understand its power and purpose. For individuals who fall in love hard and fast, it's a waterfall of emotions that takes us from one whirlpool of existence to another—fast and hard.

Although it feels good, we lose ourselves—it's like quicksand.

We cannot do much about the emotions pouring through us about the person we've fallen for because we're also fighting off the anxiety and fear of them leaving us. This fear is often accompanied by the joy in hope, that they are the person who will fulfill our visions of having a prospering soul mate.

Often they are not. And one day, they leave.

It's devastating, and the body is put into shock as if it got hit by a ton of bricks.

We're paralyzed. Bed or dead seems best until it passes—if it chooses. The best thing that could happen is that the Heartbreaker comes knocking on our door with an apology. Or someone comes to save us with their care, and it's tenfold.

Often, though, no one saves you. It sucks. Life must go on because there are bills to pay and kids to feed.

After that, love will never be the same. People are people, and they often change their minds.

Assholes.

Love is no mistake; however, you must accept that it's a fight of faith worth taking. You also must understand the appropriate battles and swords to fight with—because love is a hell of a drug to consume.

Take heartbreaks as a way to sharpen your tool of love. When it's refined, you'll be dangerous. No one will fuck with you.

No, not one.

What once held you in bed spouting tears of dread now lifts you higher than the mountains a heartbreak once bred.

We, humans, do not fly but did you know we defied that rule by sharpening the Laws of Lift? If you are hurt, then soon, you will be lifted. And that may seem impossible—but impossible is temporary.

Whosoever hurt you did so and manifested a storm. But recognizing the chaos a storm creates, which isn't there to muddy your path but rather to clear it, clarifies what your tool needs.

Your purpose is higher than providing love for hell-bent hearts. Time heals all wounds. But only if you use time to heal.

Let go or be dragged.

∞

Go Or Die

March 31, 2022

For why are there forbidden places—spaces they warn not to go? Street signs indicating danger is ahead—keep exploring; it may just be your head.

We must be kids, however, carefully… We must allow our children to adventure, but carefully.

Humans have only explored less than 20 percent of the oceans. Greater than 80 percent is uncharted. It's vast, powerful, and with immense pressures at the depths, LORD knows what the human mind has yet to see down there. There are several reasons ships don't sail through some ocean regions. It's choppy, rocky, and never doubt the unknown territorial species.

Let's say you become the curious child and go where you're warned not to. LORD knows what lies ahead for you. The environment at first is welcoming because it's likely curious of you. The guardians and leaders of the land watch conspicuously as you explore, touching, smelling, and tasting. Since it's 2022, you capture the moments with the technology you are pleased to do so with.

You get away with it once, twice, and a third. Now you feel accepted. But unmapped territory, uncharted land, and the unknown organisms don't consider feelings when they must let you know you've crossed their line.

The ignorant don't make it back to share their part of the dangerous exploration. The inconsiderate are lucky enough to still have their tongues to tell their story. And for the wise, they're the reasons we know not to explore these areas.

Whether it's land, water, or space above, a warning about the unknown is just words at first. The wise men who witness the inconsiderate are shown where the ignorant bodies are placed.

But do the wise not listen? Or are they chosen because it's their purpose to explore danger, yet carefully?

LORD knows.

For the ignorant are given the journey in an attempt to make it theirs. For the inconsiderate, they make the journey to share what's there. And for the wise, they only need to see it once.

The wise do not walk in danger for views; they walk in danger for you. Therefore, the sun will only rise on the chosen journeying few.

Do as the wise say, not as they do.

∞

Depths Of Me

April 4, 2022

Do you think the river waters have any heads up of the bends ahead? When the course of the river changes, water does, too, flowing as the ripples of the surface must adjust as well. Water will never assume its stillness is eternal, or the falls are a consequence of nature.

Bodies of water, vast and dangerous, reap havoc for those who don't respect its changing conditions. For it freezes when below zero and boils above 212 degrees Fahrenheit. Most boats are engineered beautifully enough to float in the ocean—but please, find it mysterious that only 20 percent of earth's waters have been explored. And so, I've said it here before, we know nothing of the oceans. But we know the rivers.

Rivers are safe, predictable, and contained by land. Some rivers will flood land, causing catastrophic damage to cities, communities, and death. That's the nature of water.

The human body is roughly 70 percent water. Do you think we have a high tide version of ourselves during a full moon? And like rapids through a river, does our anxiety cause chaos for others around us? Do we have unexplored territories within us that will never be unfolded because we're vast in our conscious abilities, or vigorously unpredictable when dependent upon our primitive instincts?

These questions have been answered by scientists, philosophers, spiritual leaders, and individuals who have explored their internal souls beyond a conditionally contained environment.

You cannot define water within a river, lake, or pond, nor in the ocean, because it freezes and boils, too. But water becomes the ocean once it's poured into the sea. Once its environment heats up, it becomes a gas. Once its surroundings freeze, it becomes solid.

It can always go back to the rivers, assuming that's where it came from. But it will never be the same. The water will be salty, sandy, or contaminated. That's life—it's a beach.

If anyone fears the unexplored, remain in the rivers. The deep ocean is for those willing to risk the pressures of a paradigm shift. Those who return in fear become the gardener in a war. Those who return untethered become the destined *protective-warrior* of their garden. Why do you think they explored deep oceans in the first place?

One answer is, they never forget the rivers before.

∞

Wonder Wall

April 21, 2022

Slowly, is the fastest way to get where you desire to be.

Whether it's depicted through moods or external validations, you will experience periods of exponential growth—where you cycle between emotions of highs to lows. Your lows, however, through time, or you, will be 'higher type' lows than the lows experienced before.

Your conditioning with these lows will often be associated with the feelings of your past lows, so you won't feel as though you're progressing. It's like taking four steps forward, then two steps back. And another four steps forward and three steps back. From there, six steps forward and three steps back.

Cumulative progress over time will make it evident that you've progressed further from your original starting point. Once you understand that, you'll understand that emotions on all levels are relative and, for the most part, similar by their degree of experience.

It's like driving on a winding road to success, a person, or thing you desire. As most will associate their emotions to past circumstances, which deceives you into thinking you're stuck, it's the reason people give up.

Become a bit delusionally insane. And that's why I write—to tell you there's no such thing as turning back.

The reason to move slow is to learn self-compassion. It's also a great idea to allow your body and mind to sync after the upgrade. From there, you can proceed in terms of showing off what you learned—the mind will ruminate faster than the body.

This is why you must shut up and write.

Once you're past the patterns of emotions, you become untouchable—and that's non-negotiable. Think of it like riding a bicycle; you must keep paddling forward to sustain your balance.

Movement is key.

If you find yourself sitting too long or indecisive, you may get attacked by negative thoughts. So remember, you cannot think yourself into positive action; you must act yourself into positive thinking.

The road may be dark, but movement in faith is the light.

∞

Hymn To Sun

April 24, 2022

Over the waters it sings,
Splashing molecules, recedes,
Word by word some blinding,
But through meaning they're binding,
A shining light which finds me,
In places I write beast,
...soo much the sun stares me,
Calling toward the east, pulling means at ease,
Saying, "Write me, write me..."
I respond, "Show me, show me..."
There, it implores me, grows me, and ignites me.
Here, you can see me, read me—a free me,
But that's arbitrary,
You wouldn't get me,
Free is damming, disciplining,
Yet shinning, & confining.
But regal in its nature,
Plain like paper,
Tasteless as,
Water,
Sun,
Now,
You sea...

∞

Resting Feet

April 26, 2022

Hello from the other side. It's the area of which you don't reside. The land of the disciplined and those who can't decide. Here, there are no troubles or pains—and the uncertainty is like cocaine. Not the party drug, but the inner hits of dopamayne.

If you're trying to make sense of what's written, don't, you can't, because we're not listening to the same tunes.

We're not sipping the same cup of bitter Masala tea. So even if you try, you'll fail to render the idea that you're confined to your rivers.

This, was written from the seas of life—where an infinite school of words drift from between the seabed to the surface. Some words taken aboard, some rejected, and so what…

Assuming you swim upon these waters, you know one thing—it sucks. Often in no man's land, it can seem like days, weeks, or months before swimming upon new shores of meaning. The wise who claim they've made it, suggest that enjoying the journey is most important, because the destination is one point in time which passes. And so is each moment en route.

Consider this, the voyage and destination are one. Once you understand that, you invite yourself to the first cardinal rule of life.

There's no journey to complete, so rest your feet. This is a dance, my boy… Take your time.

∞

Uptown Muse

May 9, 2022

What lies inside your favorite songs, is what lies inside of you.
It's the glorious view, of a potential new you.
Whoever creates the art, takes the muse.
Whoever takes the muse, strengthens the art.
Whoever gives the art, shares the muse.
How is a muse elated?
How can a muse be translated?
They'll tell you that music is the vernacular of the soul;
Words transcribe the meaning of desire, passion—
And the happening grit humans hold in vain.
If a muse becomes a person, that person is a tool.
If a muse is misused, that user is a fool.
They wrote, "Don't cast your pearls before swine."
But today, swine dances to foolish pearls.
So, what did they put in your favorite songs?
Go listen—only fools miss it.

∞

Pure Imagination

June 4, 2022

To imagine is to plan. To plan is to write. To write is to act.

Acting is embodying imagination through expression. From a string of events being carried out to small tasks accomplished through time, embodying imagination brings out inner visions by a love language called 'acts of service.'

This is important because it's transactional.

Imagination can be strung in either direction, from worst-case scenarios to visions of someone's highest hopes and dreams. What steers these mindful visions is mainly based on someone's lifestyle conditioning.

Trauma can suppress the ability to imagine; therefore, these people must seek therapy to heal these parts of their mind. Lifestyle habits and circumstances can also hinder imagination because trauma and habits are often processed the same in the brain.

The brain does not store neutral memories. So, you may be unaware of what negative patterns are holding you back. Therefore, therapy is highly recommended if you feel your imagination is bad or impeded.

The law of attraction does not exist without 'action.' If the impulsive actions are not carried out, your imagination will be just that—a still image.

Personally, I do not advocate for the law of attraction, but like the laws of power, laws of polarity, laws of relativity, and laws of correspondence, ignorance of their patterns enables their existence.

Leonardo da Vinci quotes, "There are three classes of people: those who see, those who see when they are shown, and those who do not see."

Imagination will always be of the mind. Creativity is the ability to produce it.

∞

Mary Coen

June 11, 2022

What is a miracle?

Something extraordinary. A chain of events science and nature cannot explain. Or, you.

Why don't we see miracles often?

Miracles of biblical times were conditional. They were written as 'parables,' meaning the actual events related to the happenings were *paired* by a writer's best *ability* to explain them.

Today, they're talked about because it's allowed within the vain of our existence. Other animals don't care about that shit.

Who will create miracles?

You.

When are miracles created?

As soon as you expect one to happen.

Since science or nature cannot explain most 'miracles', a phenomenon must be strung out by you, the miracle curator.

A magician is just that—someone puppeteering illusions through the mind—but only to those who won't get it. When your miracle arrives, let it be a miracle to those who won't understand your narrative and purpose.

They would never guess you wrote the blueprint to the magic unfolding.

If you're confused, space is granted to write it out.

∞

Benedictus

July 13, 2022

I've seen it all,
Cover your eyes, if you may.
But no, it's July,
Who lied?
Now until fall,
I give it my all,
…that won't be all,
Til' my new call,
Pick it up,
That a string, I am,
Stricken flute,
Blowing for you,
Resting now,
.
.
.
From the vernacular of souls,
Chanting, it grows.
We called it—bamboo strolls.
Drums a beat, opening eyes,
In peace, we speak,
Each ear so pleased.
Thank the conductor.
It's you, so…
Don't seek.

∞

HACE TUTO GUAGUA

August 23, 2022

To this song, it came to me—
An everlasting asking,
My future, my comfort,
And to hold your aspirations,
I sleep in faith.
To this song, it called me—
My infinite request,
My path, my security,
And to pursue your trust.
To this hymn, you found me—
An internal hum,
Your voice, my ear,
And to arrive at your secret,
I rest, you watch,
A child's song.

∞

Listening Journal

September 24, 2022

There are many songs that'll meet me en route to you, book two.

As I stay connected, embedded in my roots of youth, these sounds and our artists will send me tunes—I'll cruise, I'll muse…

A song or two a day will keep the writer awake. Some rap, some flutes, or maybe alternative acoustical blues.

Exploring the sounds of a song is like swimming in the deep ends of creation, existence, and hidden pathways most avoid. And then you feel them, but only if you care to.

It can get weird—scary, too.

Personally, I've become open to the visions, embracive of the emotions—I do all but deny.

Three years ago I hated Lo-Fi. Today, it's become the genre I often journal to. Five years ago, I could care less for Enya. However, one by one, song by song, I muse into new voyages through her new aging vocals.

So until the next toe tapper, I'm chin up and listening loudly so it can get all up in ya…That is, a new book, a new story, and what I once coined an uphill run on the hilltops of glory.

∞

www.ingramcontent.com/pod-product-compliance
Lightning Source LLC
LaVergne TN
LVHW010624100826
845148LV00014B/3091

* 9 7 8 1 7 3 3 2 1 7 2 4 8 *